A LOOK AT PRIMARY SOURCES

PHOTOGRAPHS

BY KRISTEN RAJCZAK NELSON

Gareth Stevens
PUBLISHING

CRASHCOURSE

Please visit our website, www.garethstevens.com. For a free color catalog of all our high-quality books, call toll free 1-800-542-2595 or fax 1-877-542-2596.

Library of Congress Cataloging-in-Publication Data
Names: Rajczak Nelson, Kristen, author.
Title: Photographs / Kristen Rajczak Nelson.
Description: Buffalo : Gareth Stevens Publishing, [2024] | Series: A look at primary sources | Includes index.
Identifiers: LCCN 2022059232 (print) | LCCN 2022059233 (ebook) | ISBN 9781538287569 (library binding) | ISBN 9781538287552 (paperback) | ISBN 9781538287576 (ebook)
Subjects: LCSH: Photography in historiography--Juvenile literature. | History--Sources--Juvenile literature.
Classification: LCC D16.155 .R35 2024 (print) | LCC D16.155 (ebook) | DDC 907.2022/2--dc23/eng/20230109
LC record available at https://lccn.loc.gov/2022059232
LC ebook record available at https://lccn.loc.gov/2022059233

First Edition

Published in 2024 by
Gareth Stevens Publishing
2544 Clinton Street
Buffalo, NY 14224

Designer: Claire Wrazin
Editor: Kristen Rajczak Nelson

Photo credits: Cover (photo), pp. 5 (Empire State Building), 11 (bottom), 13 (top and bottom), 17 (photo) Everett Collection/Shutterstock.com; series art (background texture) Verbena/Shutterstock.com; series art (cover typeface) Gleb Guralnyk/Shutterstock.com; series art (photo frame) Nataliia K/Shutterstock.com; p. 4 (photo) File:Raising_the_Flag_on_Iwo_Jima.png/Wikimedia Commons; pp. 5 (bottom left), 11, 15, 17 (letter), 21 Courtesy of Library of Congress; p. 5 (bottom right) Luciano Mortula - LGM/Shutterstock.com; p. 7 File:Civil_Rights_March_on_Washington,_D.C._(Leaders_of_the_march_leading_marchers_down_the_street.)_-_NARA_-_542003.tif/Wikimedia Commons; p. 9 Division of Work and Industry, National Museum of American History, Smithsonian Institution; p. 17 (newspaper article) File:Telegram_extra._Assassination_of_Abraham_Lincoln/Wikimedia Commons; p. 19 Wirestock Creators/Shutterstock.com; p. 23 PreciousPhotos/Shutterstock.com; p. 25 Ground Picture/Shutterstock.com; p. 27 Stock Holm/Shutterstock.com; p. 29 Salma Bashir Motiwala/Shutterstock.com; p. 29 (photo frame) Hintau Aliaksei/Shutterstock.com

Printed in the United States of America

CPSIA compliance information: Batch #CS24GS: For further information contact Gareth Stevens at 1-800-542-2595.

CONTENTS

Words in the glossary appear in **bold** type the first time they are used in the text.

TAKE A PICTURE!

Photographs are the pictures made by a camera. For many years, cameras used **film** to capture, or record, photos. Today, many photos are **digital**! A photograph can be used as a primary source no matter what form it's in.

MAKE THE GRADE

The first photograph was taken in France in 1826.

FIRSTHAND PHOTOS

A primary source is a firsthand source. It was created, or made, by a person who **witnessed** an event, or something that happened. It was created during a time that is being studied. Primary sources give **details** that might not have been known otherwise.

MARCH ON WASHINGTON FOR JOBS AND FREEDOM
AUGUST 28, 1963

MAKE THE GRADE

A secondary source uses primary sources and other facts to interpret, or give the meaning of, something about an event or time period.

FOR EVERYONE

Taking a photo used to take a long time and cost a lot. Photos were often **posed**. Over time, photography became faster, cheaper, and more common. By the 1900s, many people owned cameras! They took photos of their families. Photography became an art.

MAKE THE GRADE

In 1888, the Kodak company introduced a camera for everyday people.

ORIGINAL KODAK CAMERA

DOCUMENTING HISTORY

Photos are helpful primary sources to use when studying history. They have **documented** important events and time periods. The **Civil War** was the first war during which many photographs were taken. The photos show what life was like for soldiers and the effects of battle.

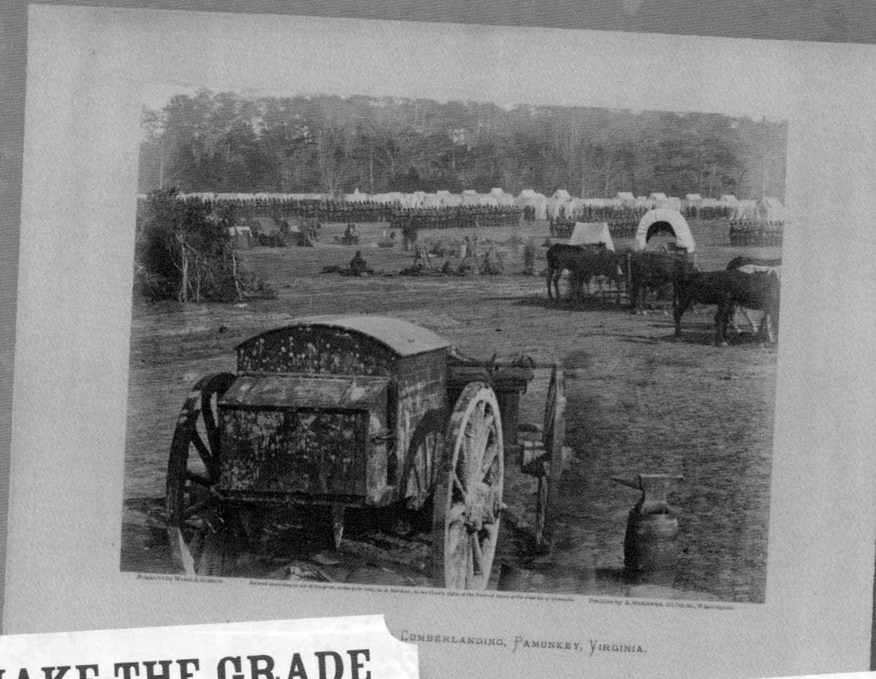

MAKE THE GRADE

Photographers followed the Northern army during the Civil War. Their photos brought the war into Americans' homes.

Historic photographs show the lives of everyday people. Photos show what people wore and how they did their hair. Photos show the jobs people spent their time doing, such as tending fields, washing clothes, or working in a factory.

MAKE THE GRADE

Photos show what words may not be able to **express.** Photos of children working in factories may give someone a stronger feeling than simply reading about it.

Photographs can be important primary sources to learn about cultures. Some groups of people have no written records. Photographs of them might be the only way to learn about them. Photos also may show **traditional** clothing and **customs**.

MAKE THE GRADE

Culture is the beliefs and ways of life of a group of people.

GET THE CONTEXT

Photographs capture a moment in time. However, in order to understand them, more historical **context** is often needed. They are usually used with other primary sources such as letters or diaries to get a full picture of a time or event.

PRESIDENT ABRAHAM LINCOLN, FEBRUARY 1865

Executive Mansion,

Washington, Aug. 23, 1

This morning, as for some day[s]
past, it seems exceedingly pro[b]-
ably that this Administration w[ill]
not be re-elected. Then it will
be my duty to so co-operate with
the ~~Government~~ President elect,
as to save the Union between the
election and the inauguration; as
he will have secured his election
on such ground that he cannot
possibly save it afterwards.

A. Lincoln.

35496

LETTER WRITTEN BY LINCOLN

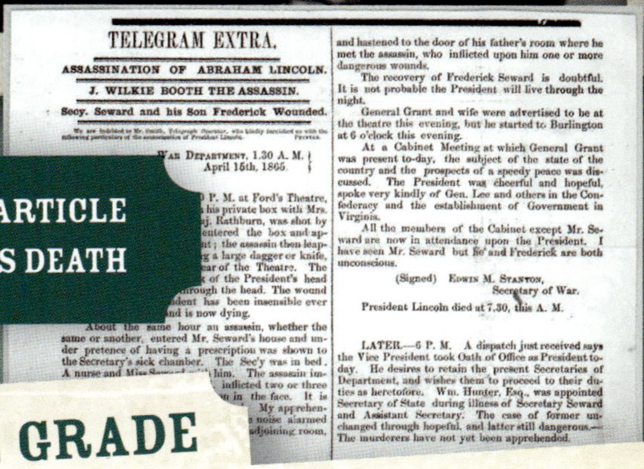

TELEGRAM EXTRA.

ASSASSINATION OF ABRAHAM LINCOLN.

J. WILKIE BOOTH THE ASSASSIN.

Secy. Seward and his Son Frederick Wounded.

War Department, 1.30 A. M.
April 15th, 1865.

... P. M. at Ford's Theatre, ... his private box with Mrs. ...j. Rathburn, was shot by ... entered the box and ap- ...t; the assassin then leap- ...g a large dagger or knife, ...ear of the Theatre. The ...k of the President's head ...hrough the head. The wound ...ident has been insensible ever ...nd is now dying.

About the same hour an assassin, whether the same or another, entered Mr. Seward's house and under pretence of having a prescription was shown to the Secretary's sick chamber. The Sec'y was in bed. A nurse and Miss Seward ... him. The assassin ... inflicted two or three ... in the face. It is ... My apprehen- ... noise alarmed ... adjoining room, and hastened to the door of his father's room where he met the assassin, who inflicted upon him one or more dangerous wounds.

The recovery of Frederick Seward is doubtful. It is not probable the President will live through the night.

General Grant and wife were advertised to be at the theatre this evening, but he started to Burlington at 6 o'clock this evening.

At a Cabinet Meeting at which General Grant was present to-day, the subject of the state of the country and the prospects of a speedy peace was discussed. The President was cheerful and hopeful, spoke very kindly of Gen. Lee and others in the Confederacy and the establishment of Government in Virginia.

All the members of the Cabinet except Mr. Seward are now in attendance upon the President. I have seen Mr. Seward but he and Frederick are both unconscious.

(Signed) Edwin M. Stanton,
Secretary of War.

President Lincoln died at 7.30, this A. M.

LATER.—6 P. M. A dispatch just received says the Vice President took Oath of Office as President to-day. He desires to retain the present Secretaries of Department, and wishes them to proceed to their duties as heretofore. Wm. Hunter, Esq., was appointed Secretary of State during illness of Secretary Seward and Assistant Secretary. The case of former unchanged through hopeful, and latter still dangerous.—The murderers have not yet been apprehended.

NEWSPAPER ARTICLE ABOUT LINCOLN'S DEATH

MAKE THE GRADE

Knowing when and where a photo was taken helps the viewer understand what they are seeing.

WHAT'S THE MESSAGE?

Historians, or people who study history, look for clues in a photograph to figure out the photographer's message or purpose for taking the photograph. The largest or clearest person or thing in a photo is often the photographer's main subject.

AFTERMATH OF HURRICANE KATRINA
BILOXI, MISSISSIPPI
SEPTEMBER 6, 2005

MAKE THE GRADE

A photographer who works for a newspaper or website may take hundreds of photos. Only a few are chosen to be shared with the public.

A photograph's composition, or how it's made up, includes how close the photographer is to the subject of the photo. A close-up photo makes the viewer feel like they are there. A photo taken from far away gives the viewer a sense of a whole scene.

MAKE THE GRADE

Photographers choose what to show—and not show—in a photo they are taking. Why they made that choice can be part of understanding these primary sources.

Photographers choose what to photograph and how to do it. Photographers may want the viewer to feel or act a certain way once they see it. Photos of people without much food may push a viewer to give food or money to those in need of help.

MAKE THE GRADE

Photographs of war have often changed what the public thinks about the war.

Photographs may show a photographer's bias or the bias of the newspaper or magazine it's in. Bias includes the beliefs that one person, group, or idea is better than others. Bias is another reason photos are considered with other sources when studying history.

MAKE THE GRADE

Photographs, especially digital ones, can be edited, or changed. These changes can include changing the color or cutting out part of a scene.

PRIMARY SOURCES TODAY

Many historical photos have been digitized, or made into computer files, so anyone can look at them online. This keeps the original photos safe from wear. Historical photos seen online or in a book can still be used as primary sources.

MAKE THE GRADE

Places that show items from history like museums, colleges, and libraries, collect historic photos and other primary sources for us to learn from.

Today, anyone with a smartphone can take a picture! These too can be primary sources. More and more, everyday people are witnessing events and capturing them in photographs. Someday, these will be used by those studying our time in history!

PRESIDENT BARACK OBAMA AND KING ABDULLAH BIN ABDUL AZIZ OF SAUDI ARABIA

MAKE THE GRADE

Photographs can show the relationship between two people, or how they are connected.

USING A PHOTOGRAPH AS A PRIMARY SOURCE

This activity can be done with a historic photograph found in the Library of Congress online collection or even an old family photo!

Choose a photograph.

- *What does it show?*
- *How does it make you feel?*

Find out the following, if you can:

- *When was it taken?*
- *Who took the photo?*
- *Why did they take the photo?*

Look at the composition. Is it a close-up or taken from far away?

- *Why do you think the photographer made that choice?*
- *How would a different composition change your interpretation of the photo?*
- *Is there anything missing from the photo that may have been edited out or just not shown?*

Find out more about the photo by looking up other primary sources. This can include talking to a family member who was there!

Write a paragraph summing up your first thoughts about the photo and how they changed as you spent time studying it.

GLOSSARY

Civil War: A war fought from 1861 to 1865 in the United States between the Union (the Northern states) and the Confederacy (the Southern states).

context: The surrounding conditions.

custom: A way of doing things that is usual among the people in a certain group or place.

detail: A small part of something.

digital: Using or having to do with computers.

document: To create a record of.

express: To make known.

film: A material used for taking photographs.

pose: To sit, stand, or lie down for a photograph to be taken.

traditional: Having to do with past actions or ways of life.

witness: To see happen.

FOR MORE INFORMATION

BOOKS

Boswell, Kelly. *Research Primary Source Documents: Diaries, Letters, Journals, and More!*. North Mankato, MN: Pebble, 2019.

Davies, Monika. *Photographs Throughout American History.* New York, NY: Gareth Stevens Publishing, 2020.

WEBSITE

Classroom Materials at the Library of Congress
www.loc.gov/classroom-materials/?fa=partof_type:primary+source+set
Check out the Library of Congress's sets of primary sources, including historic photographs, here.

Publisher's note to educators and parents: Our editors have carefully reviewed these websites to ensure that they are suitable for students. Many websites change frequently, however, and we cannot guarantee that a site's future contents will continue to meet our high standards of quality and educational value. Be advised that students should be closely supervised whenever they access the internet.

INDEX